SERVICE DOGS

by Linda Tagliaferro

Consultant: Wilma Melville, Founder
National Disaster Search Dog Foundation

New York, New York

Special thanks to Wilma Melville who founded the:
National Disaster Search Dog Foundation
206 N. Signal Street, Suite R
Ojai, CA 93023
(888) 4K9-HERO
www.SearchDogFoundation.org

The Search Dog Foundation is a not-for-profit organization that rescues dogs, gives them professional training, and partners them with firefighters to find people buried alive in disasters. They produce the most highly trained search dogs in the nation.

DEDICATION: *The author would like to thank the following people for their generous help with the research for this book: Valerie Brugger of International Hearing Dog, Inc.; Jo Anne Cohn and Julie Diamond of Canine Companions for Independence; Rachel Friedman, service dog trainer; Laura Goldman, owner of service dogs Razz and Shayna; Lynn Hoover, service dog trainer and consultant; Jorjan Powers of the Assistance Dog Institute; and Lianne Rogers of Loving Paws Assistance Dogs.*

Design and production by Dawn Beard Creative and Octavo Design and Production, Inc.

Credits

Cover, Front (left), Image Source / Fotosearch; (top right), International Hearing Dog, Inc.; (center right), Spencer Grant / Photo Edit; (bottom right), Canine Companions for Independence; Back (top), International Hearing Dog, Inc.; (center), Spencer Grant / Photo Edit; (bottom), Canine Companions for Independence. Title page, Image Source / Fotosearch. Page 3, Canine Companions for Independence; 4-5, Jeff Tuttle / The Wichita Eagle Newspaper; 5(top), International Hearing Dog, Inc.; 5(bottom), International Hearing Dog, Inc.; 6, International Hearing Dog, Inc.; 6-7, Unicorn Stock Photo; 8, Canine Companions for Independence; 8-9 A. Ramey/Unicorn Stock Photos; 10-11(both), The Assistance Dog Institute; 12-13, Spencer Grant / Photo Edit; 14, neal and molly jansen / Alamy; 15, Tom Nebbia / CORBIS; 16-17, Canine Companions for Independence; 17, AP / Wide World Photos; 18-19, Ken Sergi; 19, AP / Wide World Photos; 20-21, 22-23, Canine Companions for Independence; 24-25, Frank Siteman / Rainbow; 26-27, Doug DuKane; 27, Canine Companions for Independence; 29(top), PhotoSpin.com; 29(bottom), Photodisc / Fotosearch; 30, Tom Nebbia / CORBIS.

Library of Congress Cataloging-in-Publication Data

Tagliaferro, Linda.
  Service dogs / by Linda Tagliaferro ; consultant, Wilma Melville.
    p. cm. — (Dog heroes)
  Includes bibliographical references and index.
  ISBN 1-59716-016-4 (lib. bdg.) — ISBN 1-59716-039-3 (pbk.)
  1. Service dogs—Juvenile literature. 2. Hearing ear dogs—Juvenile literature.
  I. Melville, Wilma. II. Title. III. Series.

HV1569.6.T34 2005
362.4'0483—dc22

                        2004021060

For more information, write to Bearport Publishing Company, Inc., 101 Fifth Avenue, Suite 6R, New York, New York 10003. Printed in the United States of America in North Mankato, Minnesota.

042011
040111CGC

10 9 8 7 6 5 4

Table of Contents

Danger Ahead!

Betty Sims didn't know her life was in danger. A **tornado** was headed toward her house in Kansas. Betty is deaf. She couldn't hear what was happening outside. Her dog Tykie, however, heard loud noises that sounded like a rushing train.

Dogs can hear almost four times better than humans. Dogs can also hear sounds that humans can't hear at all.

Tykie jumped up and touched Betty's leg. He raced to the window and Betty followed. Suddenly, she saw the storm. She grabbed Tykie and ran into a closet. Seconds later, the tornado hit. The front of Betty's house exploded into pieces. The closet, however, was safe. Tykie had saved Betty's life.

Tykie

Betty Sims' house after the tornado

The tornado that destroyed Betty Sims' house caused damage in many areas of Wichita, Kansas.

Trained to Serve

Tykie was taught to **alert** his deaf owner to sounds that she can't hear. Tykie is a **service** dog. Dogs such as Tykie are trained to help people who have medical problems. These problems can make it hard for them to do some everyday things.

Some service dogs wear special capes to show that they are working dogs.

A service dog, for example, may help people in wheelchairs. He can pick up a ringing telephone with his mouth and carry it to his human **partner**. Some dogs press elevator buttons. Others carry wallets. Service dogs learn to do some pretty amazing things for their human friends.

A service dog helping out

Going Everywhere

Service dogs live with their partners and go everywhere with them. Travis goes to work with Ellen, a doctor. Ellen's **patients** love the dog. At home, Travis takes clothes out of the dryer. He gets a drink for Ellen. It's hard for Ellen to do these things from her wheelchair.

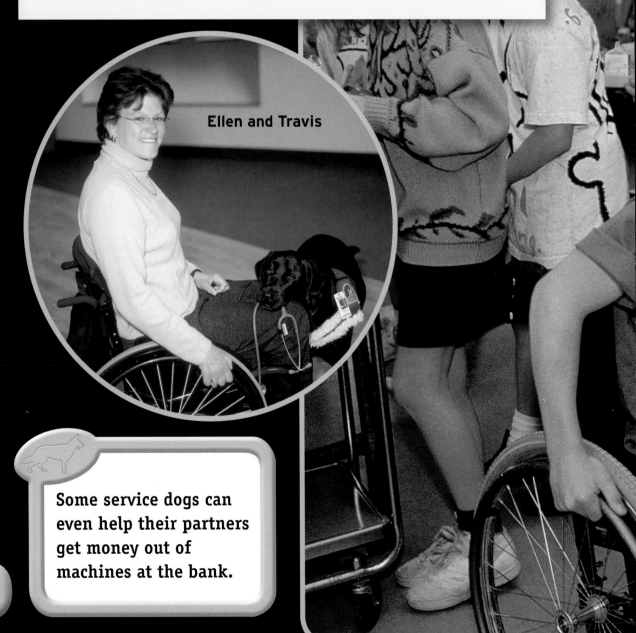

Ellen and Travis

Some service dogs can even help their partners get money out of machines at the bank.

Service dogs can even go to school with their partners. They are able to ride the school bus and sit in a classroom with the children. These animals are trained to stay calm and sit still.

A Puppy at Work

Bonnie Bergin first came up with the idea of using dogs to help people with health problems. In 1974, she visited Nepal, a country in Asia. She saw people who had trouble walking. They leaned on donkeys for help. When she returned home, she began teaching dogs to help people walk.

Abdul shakes hands with Kerry Knaus. Kerry was the first person to receive a "Canine Companion" service dog.

Bonnie first worked with a woman who could not move most of her body. Together, they trained a puppy named Abdul. They taught him to pick up things. Abdul learned quickly. In 1975, Bonnie started a group to train service dogs. She called the group **Canine Companions for Independence**.

Bonnie Bergin

In 1979, Agnes McGrath started a group to train dogs to help deaf people. The group is called International Hearing Dog, Inc.

Best Breeds

Labrador retrievers and golden retrievers are friendly dogs that are strong, calm, and faithful. They like to find things and bring them to people. They make good helpers for people in wheelchairs who need things picked up and brought to them.

Service dogs sleep in the same bedroom as their partners. Often a dog bed is placed beside the partner's bed.

Many **breeds** of dog can become alert dogs for people with epilepsy, a brain **disease**. This disease causes people to suddenly fall down and shake. Some dogs can tell when someone with epilepsy is about to get sick. They bark to warn the person to sit down in a safe place.

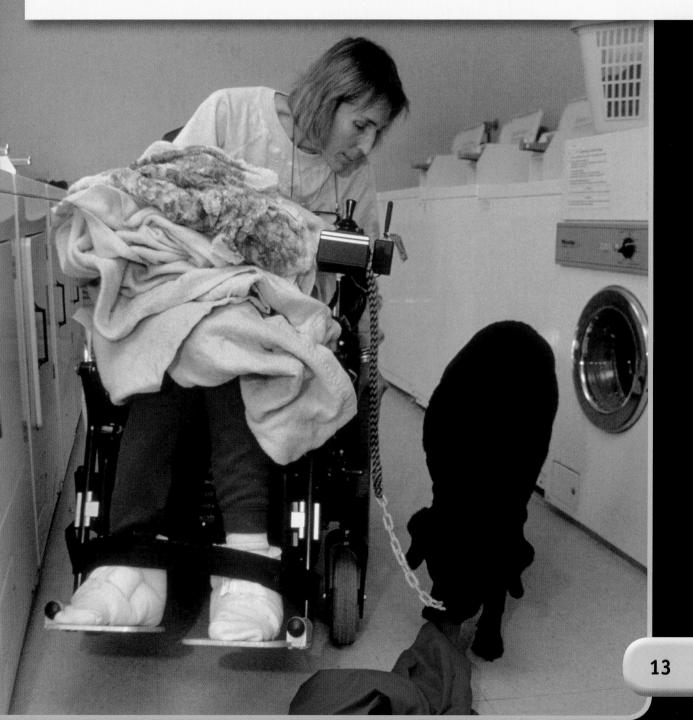

Training Tales

A service dog must be healthy. An animal doctor at a training school checks his heart, ears, and hips when he's eight weeks old. If he's well, the puppy moves in with people who will care for him. These people are puppy raisers. They teach the puppy to **obey**. They take him to places so he can learn about the world.

When a puppy is a year old, he leaves his puppy raiser and returns to training school. There he learns many new things. For example, he's taught how to pull a wheelchair and to turn on a light switch.

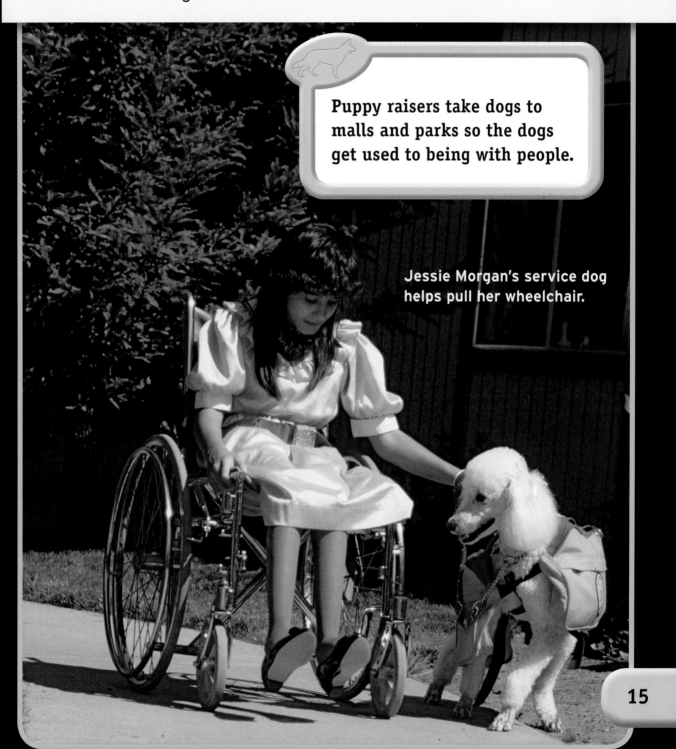

Puppy raisers take dogs to malls and parks so the dogs get used to being with people.

Jessie Morgan's service dog helps pull her wheelchair.

The Partners Meet

Service dogs must be brave and friendly. Some dogs, however, bark at cars. Others chase cats or growl at people. These animals will not make good service dogs. They have to return to their puppy raisers' home where they will live happily as pets.

Kimberly and her service dog Gino

The puppies that will make good service dogs train for six months. After that time, a puppy is ready to meet his human partner. For two weeks, the human and the dog will train as a team. The partner will learn how to take care of the dog so he will be safe and happy.

A puppy in training learns to climb up steps.

A person should never pet a service dog without first asking the dog's human partner.

Graduation Day

On **graduation** day, the puppy raisers arrive at the training school. Each one takes the leash of the dog he or she has raised. Together, they walk over to the dog's new partner. The puppy raiser hands over the leash.

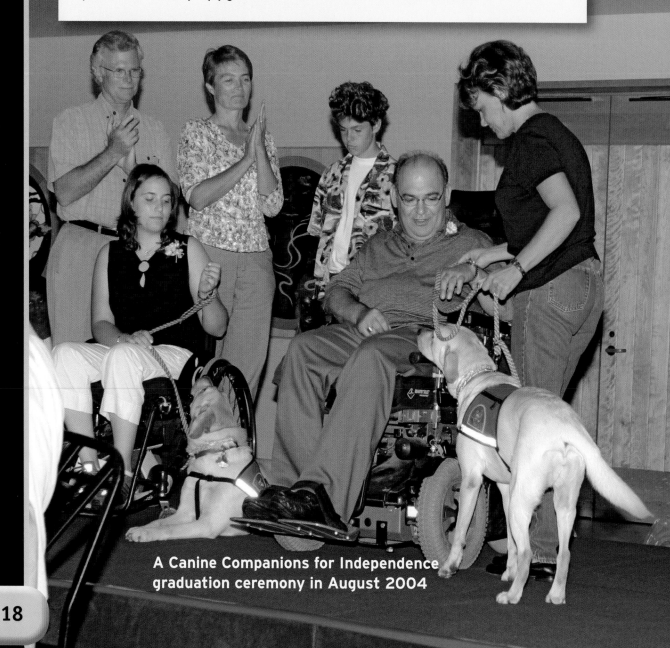

A Canine Companions for Independence graduation ceremony in August 2004

At the end of the day, the animal and his new friend go home. It's exciting for the dog to walk around the house and get to know his new family.

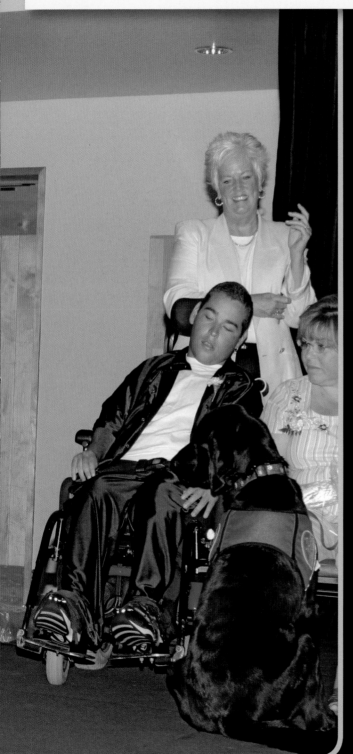

Lane Phalen and her service dog Beau at home.

Less than half of the puppies in a training program are good enough to become service dogs.

Dogs on the Job

Razz is a service dog who lives with Laura. Laura has a disease that makes her muscles weak. Sometimes she loses her balance. Razz is strong. He gently pushes against her so she doesn't fall.

Teo and Owen

It's difficult for Owen to use his arms and legs. He's lucky to have his service dog Teo to help him. Teo has learned to pull off Owen's socks. One of Owen's favorite things is to invite Teo up on the bed and read to him.

A service dog can use his mouth to carry a credit card to the store clerk.

Great Friends

Lynn can't hear well. Aniki is her service dog. Aniki softly pulls at Lynn's clothes when the doorbell rings. If Lynn drops her keys, Aniki picks them up and carries them to her. Lynn thinks of Aniki as a great friend.

Tyrone wakes up his partner, Charlie, by licking his face. Charlie has a disease that makes it hard for him to control his muscles. Tyrone brings a towel to Charlie after his bath. The dog even pulls up the blankets when Charlie goes to bed!

Hearing dogs can be small because they don't need to carry or pull heavy things.

Aniki lets Lynn know that they have a visitor.

Handle with Care

Service dogs and their partners work as a team. They look out for each other. Sometimes a person's life depends on a service dog's quickness. The animal must always carefully obey his partner's **commands**.

The partner, on the other hand, makes sure the dog stays safe. The dog relies on his friend to tell him when the street is clear so they can cross. The partner makes sure the dog doesn't get his tail caught in the elevator door.

Some service dogs know the meaning of as many as 90 commands.

Lucky Dogs

Trainers are looking for better ways to teach dogs to help people. They're training some dogs to understand written commands from people who can't speak. A service dog named Norton has learned nine commands written on cards. He understands cards that say "down" and "kiss."

Luxor is helping his partner Jacob (not shown) fish.

This dog is learning to understand written commands.

Service dogs are usually very happy. They spend all day helping the people they love. They can go to schools, restaurants, and even to the movies. Their bright eyes and wagging tails show just how happy they are to lend a "helping paw."

SIT

Some people who can't speak use computers to give commands to their service dogs. The computers say the words.

Just the Facts

- Abdul was the first service dog. He was also the first dog to visit Disneyland.

- Service dogs can be male or female.

- Service dogs must be able to help their partners when they get hurt or sick. Some companies are trying to make new telephones. A service dog will be able to touch a button to dial 9-1-1 for help.

- The law allows service dogs to go places where other dogs may not go. Service dogs may go on airplanes, in restaurants, and on buses.

- Many dogs that help people who can't hear are rescued from animal shelters.

- A service dog named Endal helped his partner when a car hit him. Endal turned the man over. He put a cell phone to his ear. Endal also covered the man with a blanket. Then he went to get help.

golden retriever

Labrador retriever

alert (uh-LURT) ready to warn someone of danger; on guard

breeds (BREEDZ) types of a certain animal

Canine Companions for Independence (KAY-nine kuhm-PAN-yuhnz FOR in-di-PEN-duhnss) a group that trains dogs to help people become independent, or not need much help from other people

commands (kuh-MANDZ) instructions given to be obeyed; orders

disease (duh-ZEEZ) a certain sickness or illness

graduation (GRAJ-oo-*ay*-shuhn) the time when someone finishes a course of study in a school

obey (oh-BAY) to follow orders

partner (PART-nur) one of two or more people who do something together

patients (PAY-shuhnts) people who are getting treatment from a doctor

service (SUR-viss) work done to help others

tornado (tor-NAY-doh) a violent, whirling column of air that looks like a dark cone-shaped cloud as it moves quickly over the land

Bibliography

Jones, Karen. "From Puppy to Lifeline: Service Dogs." *New York Times*, June 6, 2004.

O'Neil, John. "For the Disabled, Special Dogs Assume Special Duties." *New York Times*, July 27, 1999.

Read More

Duden, Jane. *Helping Paws: Service Dogs.* Logan, Iowa: Perfection Learning (1998).

Patent, Dorothy Hinshaw, and William Munoz. *The Right Job for Ira: Ira's Path from Service Dog to Guide Dog.* New York, NY: Walker & Company (2004).

Learn More Online

Visit these Web sites to learn more about service dogs:

www.assistancedog.org

www.cci.org

www.deltasociety.org/dsb000.htm

www.lovingpaws.com

Index

About the Author

Linda Tagliaferro is an award-winning writer who lives in Little Neck, New York. This is her 15th book for children. She has also written books for adults and young adults.